1950

The Lion, the Witch and the Wardrobe

1939

World War II begins

1949

Farmer Giles of Ham

1942

Joins Women's Voluntary Service

1945

World War II ends

For Sam, Clare, William, and Molly, who keep my life full of wonder;
and for Pauline, who brought so much joy to so many.

Waxwing Books titles may be purchased in bulk for educational, business, fundraising,
or sales promotional use. For information, please email Support@WaxwingBooks.com.

Waxwing Books
201 W. North River Drive, Suite 370
Spokane, WA 99201
WaxwingBooks.com

Library of Congress Control Number: 2024930762
Juvenile Nonfiction | Biography & Autobiography | Literary
ISBN 978-1-956393-15-6 (hardcover)
ISBN 978-1-956393-16-3 (ebook)

The text was set in Bembo Book MT and Montecatini.
The illustrations in this book were created with
digital tools and a few bursts of wonder.
This book was edited by Caroline Starr Rose
and copy edited by Alison Kerr Miller.
Book design by Cara Llewellyn.

Manufactured in China
RRD 10 9 8 7 6 5 4 3 2 1

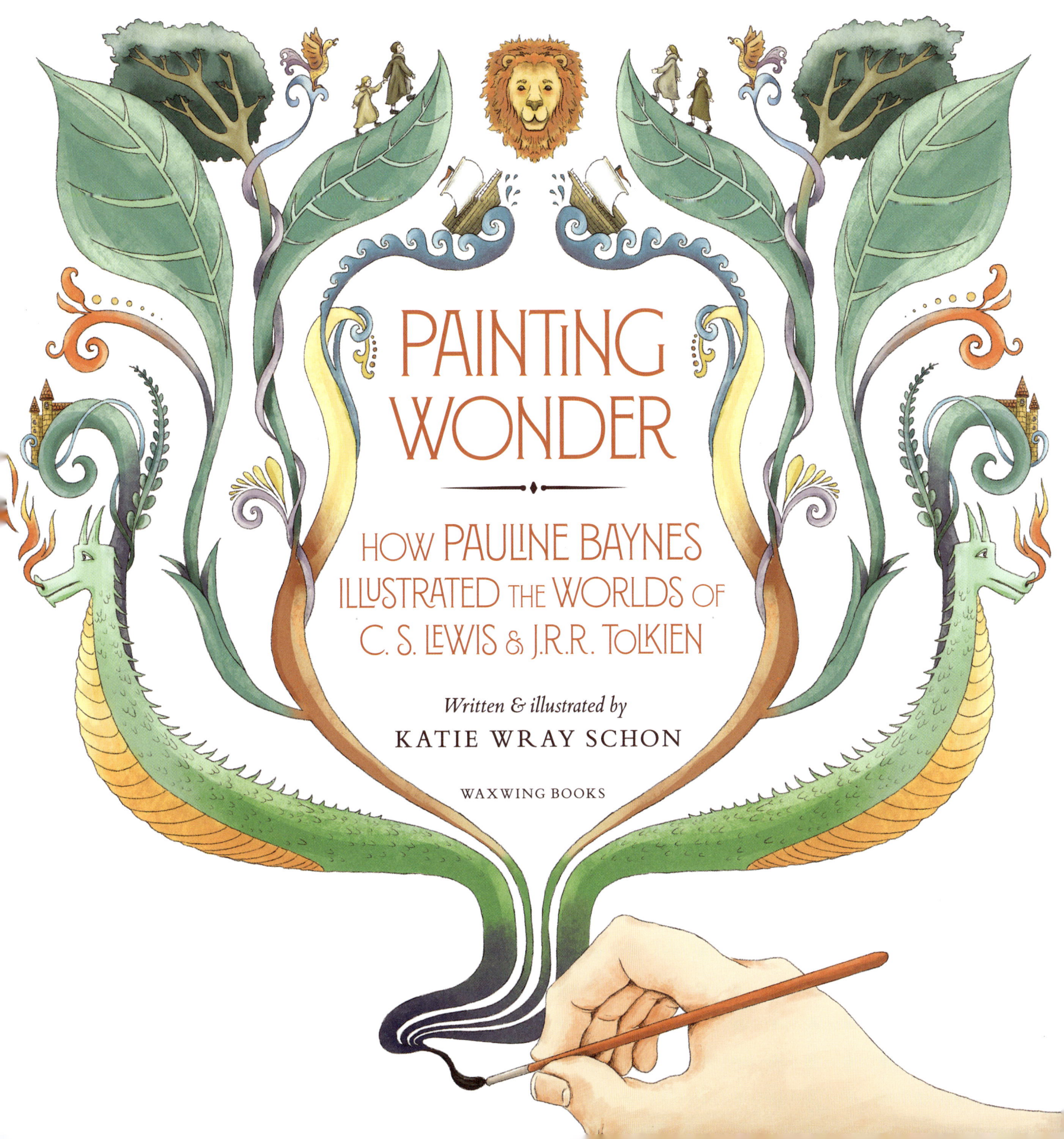

PAINTING WONDER

HOW PAULINE BAYNES ILLUSTRATED THE WORLDS OF C. S. LEWIS & J.R.R. TOLKIEN

Written & illustrated by

KATIE WRAY SCHON

WAXWING BOOKS

his little girl will grow up to draw pictures
that will wing their way around the world,
flying to faraway places.

Her pictures will be held in millions of hands—

maybe even yours.

But who is she?
And what will she draw?

Here she is at five years old.
Her childhood is filled with wonder.

She lives in a country with
towering mountains,

sparkling hidden lakes,
colorful flowers,

richly patterned saris,
loving friends and family . . .

and a monkey

trained

to take tea.

But suddenly the happy years end.

Bags in hand, she sees her saltwater tears mix with saltwater waves as the boat steams away from India and carries her . . .

. . . to England.

Boarding school.

Blackboards.

$2 + 2 =$

$3 + 5 =$

$4 + 6 =$

Bullies.

Nothing but gray.

Until . . .

a burst of wonder

breaks through the dark

from the pages of a storybook!

She swings, soars, and sails through stories,

finding friends and adventures on every new page.

Books in hand, she marches through the years,

growing,   and reading,   and growing.

And starting to draw.

A second burst of wonder—
the door to art school opens.

Paintbrush in hand, she covers
canvas after canvas with landscapes
and portraits of ladies.

She is almost an adult and
ready to start in the world
as an artist.

Then . . .

. . . World War II begins.

Bombs drop on England,

and

everyone

in

England

drops

what

they

are

doing

to

help.

Ruler and pen in hand,
she makes maps for
the navy:

bays, borders, mountains, coastlines.

Years

soldier

on.

The war ends,
and the sailors
sail home.

The people of the
world look forward
to a new start.

She looks to her past and
searches for the pieces of her
life that shine brightest.

Wonderful scenes of her childhood, beautiful books she has read,

colorful portraits she has painted.

What can she make with them all?

Pictures for books!

Pencils and pens and brushes in hand,
she makes art with a new purpose.

She draws scenes from storybooks:
dragons and dwarves,
knights and gnarled trees.

She carries her portfolio to publishers,
hoping a book will be written
that is perfect for her bright pictures.

More years go by,

as she's busy with teaching art
and caring for family
and making new friends
and waiting
and drawing
and waiting.

But all at once,
the slow years of waiting end.

A famous author,
J.R.R. Tolkien,
sees her pictures in a pile.

He wants her to draw dragons
and knights and gnarled trees
for his new book, and she does.

Her dragons fly off the page
and catch the eye of another
famous author.

He is writing about
a new magical world.

His story in hand,
she sits in front of a
blank white page.

But who is she? And what will she draw?

Her name is
Pauline Baynes.

And here is what she will draw:
Lovely landscapes and memorable
moments for the stories of **C. S. Lewis.**

Stories about a wonderful,
fantastical, magical world
called **Narnia.**

Pauline draws:
A girl
and a faun
under
an umbrella in
the snow;
a frigid
witch;
a formidable
lion;

and four children
who would save the day.

The world falls in love with Narnia,
and Pauline paints pictures for
six more books:
high mountains and hidden lakes,
waterfalls that fall up,
winged horses,
fluting fauns,
and talking animals at tea.

Years of drawing maps
give her a steady hand as she
sketches Narnia's bays and
borders, mountains
and coastlines.
J.R.R. Tolkien asks for
a map as well, to show the
way around Middle-earth,
his famous fantasy
world.

These are the pictures that wing their way around the world to faraway places on the pages of books.

They fly from past to present—

from her hands
all the way to yours.

Book in hand,

you only need
to open it a
crack

to let a burst of wonder
from Pauline's pictures
shine through.

CHILDHOOD AND BACKGROUND

Pauline Baynes was born in England in 1922, but her earliest memories were of life in India, where she lived with her family, an ayah (nanny or nursemaid) whom she loved deeply, and a pet monkey that was trained to join her at tiffin (teatime).

When Pauline was five years old, she and her sister went to England to attend boarding school. She remembered crying herself to sleep on the journey. Even with the company of her sister, Angela, Pauline struggled to find happiness at their strict boarding school. Reading was her lifeline. Rudyard Kipling was her favorite author, especially once she learned that he had also lived in India as a small child and struggled to adapt to life in England.

Pauline and her sister, who was also a talented artist, attended the same art schools. Both served the war effort when World War II began in 1940. Although it isn't shown in this story, in the early stages of the war, Pauline worked for the Royal Engineers' Camouflage Development and Training Center, likely painting models of military equipment like tanks and ships to explore methods of camouflage. While there, she met a man named Powell Perry. His family's company printed children's books, and through it, Pauline received her first commissions for picture book illustration. Later, she was sent to the Admiralty Hydrographic Department in Bath to paint maps and naval charts. During the war, she wrote and illustrated her own picture book called *Victoria and the Golden Bird*, but it wasn't until 1949, when she made illustrations for Tolkien, that Pauline became widely known.

ILLUSTRATING FOR TOLKIEN AND C. S. LEWIS

Roughly five years passed between the end of the war and Pauline's first illustrations for Tolkien. During this time, she was busy caring for her elderly parents, teaching art at the school from which she'd graduated, creating illustrations for magazines and advertisements, and building her illustration portfolio to share with publishers. There are conflicting stories about how J.R.R. Tolkien first saw Pauline's illustrations. Pauline herself said that her work was on the publisher's desk by chance, but correspondence shows that she was one of several illustrators invited to submit art for the project. Although I've shown her mailing out pictures, she may have delivered them by hand, given how difficult it would have been to make copies at the time. However he ended up seeing them, Tolkien was immediately taken by the drawings in her portfolio and was thrilled with the pictures she drew for his story.

The two continued to have a strong working relationship and friendship throughout their lives. Although she did not illustrate the Lord of the Rings books, she did create a Middle-earth map and an iconic cover for the paperback edition. She also illustrated several of Tolkien's other books.

There is also some debate about how C. S. Lewis chose Pauline Baynes to illustrate the Narnia books. Some say Tolkien recommended her directly to Lewis, who was his good friend. Another story claims Lewis walked into a bookshop and asked the bookseller for a recommendation.

How ever C. S. Lewis found her, Pauline was hired to create covers and interior drawings for *The Lion, the Witch and the Wardrobe*, and went on to illustrate the six other Narnia books. The books have been reprinted many times with new covers, yet nearly every edition of the Narnia books includes Pauline's illustrations within.

LIFE AND WORK AFTER NARNIA

Although she is certainly best known for the Narnia illustrations and her work with Tolkien, Pauline's illustration career was expansive and impressive. She won prestigious art awards, including the 1968 Kate Greenaway Medal, and created covers for *Watership Down* and some of the books in the Borrowers series. She also published illustrated versions of religious works such as Bible verses and illustrated many more picture books, chapter books, and poetry and story collections. Pauline continued illustrating until the day she passed away in 2008.

In addition to books and illustration, Pauline loved dogs. They were her primary companions, and in a way, the spark of her life's love story. One day, when she was nearly forty years old, Fritz Gasch came to her door selling dog food, and it was love at first sight. They married soon after and were very happy, but they were unable to have children. Ten years later, Fritz died, and Pauline was on her own again. She said that the years after Fritz's death were the hardest she ever experienced.

One day, she received an unexpected phone call–from Fritz's daughter! During World War II, Fritz had lost track of his family in Germany. His daughter had tracked down his whereabouts and was overjoyed to connect with Pauline. Pauline became close to Fritz's children and their children. Through them, she received the gift of a family she never thought she'd have.

"It was," she said, "like something magical coming back at me through a wardrobe."

WRITING AND ILLUSTRATING THIS BOOK

While writing and illustrating *Painting Wonder*, I ran into a lot of unknowns: What did Pauline look like as a child? What was her workspace like while she painted the Narnia pictures? Did she create most of her art with a brush, or with a pen? I don't have all of the answers, but I have done my best to use research, reminiscences from friends, and the materials they've shared to re-create Pauline's world.

I am so grateful to Pauline's friends and collectors who have helped me with this story, especially Alberto Ceccatelli, Wayne Hammond, Peter Thorpe, Brian Sibley, and Martin Springett. Thanks also to the Chapin Library at Williams College, where I spent a magical afternoon perusing their collection of Pauline Baynes' original artwork.

BIBLIOGRAPHY

"About Pauline Baynes," Pauline Baynes Tribute website, https://paulinebaynes.com/?what=about.

Bicknell, Treld, and Kaye Webb, editors, "Pauline Baynes: The Backbone Tree," *The Puffin Annual,* vol. 2. Harmondsworth, UK: Penguin Puffin, 1975.

Cory, Charlotte. "Pauline Baynes: Book Illustrator Discovered by J.R.R. Tolkien Who Went On to Create the Drawings for C. S. Lewis's Narnia Books," obituary, *Telegraph* (London), August 8, 2008.

Hammond, Wayne G. "Pauline Baynes" in *Dictionary of Literary Biography,* vol. 160: *British Children's Writers, 1914–1960.* Detroit: Gale Research, 1996.

Henshall, David. "Pauline Baynes: Witty and Inventive Children's Book Illustrator Famed for Her Narnia Drawings," obituary, *Guardian* (London), August 5, 2008.

Hooper, Walter. "*C. S. Lewis: A Companion and Guide.* New York: HarperCollins, 1996.

"Pauline Baynes: Artist and Illustrator of Narnia and Middle Earth," obituary, *Times* (London), August 9, 2008.

Sibley, Brian. "Pauline Baynes: Illustrator Who Depicted Lewis's Narnia and Tolkien's Middle-earth," obituary, *Independent* (London), August 6, 2008.

———. "Pauline Baynes: Queen of Narnia and Middle-earth," *Brian Sibley: His Blog,* August 4, 2008, http://briansibleysblog. blogspot.com/2008/08/pauline-baynes-queen-of-narnia-and.html.

Springett, Martin. "Pauline Baynes: A Remembrance by Martin Springett," *The Art and Music of Martin Springett,* http://www. martinspringett.com/paulinebaynes.html.

PHOTO CREDITS

Pauline's passport photo (previous page, left) was shared by Peter Thorpe. The other three photos were shared by Alberto Ceccatelli, Pauline's son-in-law through her marriage to Fritz Gasch.